Do not judge
any man
until you have walked
two moons
in his moccasins.

– Native American saying

The WALK THE TALK® Company

To order additional copies of this handbook or for information on other WALK THE TALK® products and services, contact us at

1.888.822.9255

or visit our website at

www.walkthetalk.com

Walk Awhile In *MY* Shoes – Healthcare Edition

Inquiries regarding permission for use of the material contained in this book should be addressed to:

The WALK THE TALK Company
2925 LBJ Freeway, Suite 201
Dallas, Texas 75234
972.243.8863

WALK THE TALK books may be purchased for educational, business, or sales promotion use.

Printed in the United States of America
10 9 8 7 6 5 4 3 2

ISBN 1-885228-43-0

Edited by Juli Baldwin and Jill Mason
Printed by MultiAd

walk awhile in *my* shoes

healthcare edition

gut-level, real-world messages
from **managers to employees**

Kathy Rice and Eric Harvey

The Authors

Kathy Rice, RPh., MBA, began her career as a staff pharmacist and currently serves as Chief Operating Officer of South Pointe Hospital – a member of the Cleveland Clinic Health System. In her 23 years at that location, she has successfully navigated her way through six job titles, three mergers, and four different hospital names. Kathy is very active in the community through Board memberships and serves as the president of the local Chamber of Commerce.

The authors dedicate this book to the outstanding people they have been privileged to work with and learn so much from.

Eric Harvey, President and CEO of the WALK THE TALK® Company, is an internationally known author, speaker, and educator in the areas of values-based business practices and organizational change. He has written twenty highly acclaimed books, including the best-selling *WALK THE TALK ... And Get The Results You Want*. With over 30 years of professional experience, Eric has held senior-level positions in numerous industries – including healthcare management.

The Publisher

Since 1977, The WALK THE TALK® Company's clear mission has been to help individuals and organizations achieve success through values-based business practices.

Besides offering an extensive library of cost-effective handbooks like this one, we specialize in providing training, consulting, and keynote presentations – all *customized* to your culture and business objectives.

Like more information? Contact our Professional Services group at **1.888.822.9255** or e-mail us at walkawhile@walkthetalk.com.

The Messages

Dear Employee:

I am every manager. I'm known by many labels: president, COO, administrator, director, department head, supervisor, team leader, boss ... and sometimes a few less flattering ones I know are used but prefer not to mention.

I am woman, and I am man. I'm every color, every belief, and every size. I'm old, young, and everything in between. I've worked here longer than you and not as long as you. I am a son. I am a daughter. I'm married and single, a parent and without children. I'm alone, and I'm surrounded by people I care about deeply.

Like you, I am a human being filled with joys, fears, frustrations, and hopes. Behind my management "game face," I feel and I laugh ... and yes, I occasionally hurt. And, like you, I want to be understood, accepted, and appreciated.

I do not believe that you can do today's job with yesterday's methods and be in business tomorrow.

– Nelson Jackson

The following pages are about opening up to you – about sharing my feelings on just a few of the many aspects of my job and how they affect me. Some of what you read may surprise you … some may bring a laugh or two. All of these pages, I hope, will encourage you to see me in a new, and perhaps much different, light.

I ask that you receive these messages with the same level of compassion and understanding that you wish from me as I read the flip side of this book. Chances are we're not as different as you may think. And just maybe, you'll be more inclined to "meet me in the middle," where we can begin a new and better working relationship.

Hear me. Understand me.

Walk awhile in *my* shoes.

on "change"

If you're expecting a lecture on the merits of change, forget it! That's not what this is about. Sure, I know that constant change is a fact of life. And yes, I fully understand that we either adapt to change or fight it in vain and watch patients go elsewhere for treatment. But in reality, many times I'm as uncomfortable and downright scared of change as you are. The healthcare market is changing so rapidly that we're ALL in uncharted waters.

Maybe you see me as the instigator or "perpetrator" of change. If you do, to a degree you're right. Sponsoring and supporting change is one of my responsibilities – and it's an absolute necessity in order to keep our organization successful and protect our jobs. But besides being a source of change, I'm also a victim of it. And when new laws, regulations, inspections, certifications, and increasing costs (just to name a few) come "rolling downhill," I end up having to make as many adjustments as anyone else. Fact is, my job changes fairly often. It seems like every six months or so, I'm "asked" to be responsible for yet another process, team, initiative, or performance-improvement project. And most times, I get nothing more for my efforts than a big "thanks" from my boss.

Like you, I have comfort zones that give me peace and a sense of stability. And just like you, my cage gets rattled when I have to change my habits by doing new and different things. Take this to the bank: **You're not the only one here who's afraid of the unknown.** Most times, I don't know what's out there any more than you do. But I do know that we have no other choice but to adapt, grow, and keep moving forward. Yes, change affects everyone. And I believe it's mostly for the good. Just look around – I think you'll find a whole bunch of changes that have turned out pretty darned positive.

So at those times when it seems like I just can't make up my mind what it is I want you to do – when each day brings a different requirement or protocol – maybe you could cut me a little slack. I'm doing the best I can. And I'm right in the middle of it ... *with* you.

When it comes to change, try walking awhile in *my* shoes!

The best managers make decisions on the basis of what is fair and equitable, not what is popular – bearing in mind that not everyone will be pleased with these decisions.

– Priscilla Gross

on making tough choices

Imagine this scenario: You've been squirreling money away, you've shopped around, and you're finally ready to buy that new high-tech TV that your family has been wanting for quite a long time. Before heading to the store, you hop in the shower, find only lukewarm water, and hop right out again. Yep, you guessed it – the water heater is on its last legs. And since funds are limited, you have to choose: Buy what everyone wants, or fix what everyone needs. The right choice is obvious, but not easy to implement because of the disappointment factor. Sound familiar? It sure does to me. I face similar (but even bigger) tough choices at work all the time.

Here's *my* typical scenario: You and your peers are wondering why we don't buy a new piece of equipment that will make life easier and help you deliver even better patient care. Well, there is a reason – it's because something called a "chiller" just broke. Heck, I don't even know what a chiller is! I just know the engineers told me we wouldn't have air conditioning if we didn't replace it. I wasn't expecting that. No one was. But since I don't want you or our patients to go without a/c, I choose to replace the chiller. It's not pretty or flashy, and no one but the engineers even knows about it. But it has to be done, so we do it. And as the new chiller purrs like a kitten, you continue to sit in the cool, comfortable air wondering why I won't buy that equipment you want. Get the picture?

When you look around and identify things we should buy or do, you usually have the luxury of focusing strictly on your particular need. I, on the other hand, am stuck with a much bigger picture to look at and lots of tradeoffs to consider. And trust me on this: Whenever funds are limited, as they are now, EVERYTHING involves tradeoffs!

That's why most of the decisions I have to make are so difficult. That's why I can't provide everything you'd like to have – even though I'd love to. That's why I'd really appreciate it if you'd walk awhile in *my* shoes.

on caring for patients

Here's something you may not know: Nothing makes me happier than watching a smiling patient leaving our facility, headed home. It reminds me of what all of us are here for: To take care of our fellow human beings. Now, here's something else you may not know: Nothing (and I mean nothing) is more disturbing to me than to hear that you sometimes think I don't care that much about patients ... that I'm only concerned with business numbers. That's simply not true. And it hurts me deeply.

The fact is, we *all* share the same goal of providing the best care possible. But we tend to view that goal from different perspectives. Admittedly, you have much more direct involvement with patients than I do. And that makes you the lucky one. Day in and day out, you're at the core of our very existence as an institution – human touch. Often, you get to see, first hand, the immediate results of all of our efforts. I envy you.

My perspective is different from yours. And, quite frankly, it's typically larger in scope, just as complicated, equally as challenging, and, often times, less rewarding. I get to do all the other stuff – like attending endless meetings, maintaining the facility, staffing, planning, coordinating with regulatory agencies, and dealing with those "business numbers" – that make it possible for you to deliver the direct care that you do so very well.

We are in the CARING BUSINESS. That's a term made up of two distinct, yet equally important and interdependent, concepts: "caring" and "business." Without the caring part, there's no need for business; without the business part, there's no opportunity for caring. You and I are partners. Each of us contributes equally to our important mission. And that's something I'd really like you to remember.

Think *you're* the only one here who gives a flip about patient care? You'll discover how untrue that is if you'll just walk awhile in *my* shoes.

Please send me extra copies of: Walk Awhile In *MY* Shoes: Healthcare Edition

1-99 copies $9.95 each   100-499 copies $8.95 each   500+ copies please call

Walk Awhile In *MY* Shoes: Healthcare Edition	____ copies X	______	=$	________
Other Recommended Resources				
Walk Awhile In *MY* Shoes	____ copies X	$ 9.95	=$	________
175 Ways To Get More Done In Less Time	____ copies X	$ 9.95	=$	________
136 Effective Presentation Tips	____ copies X	$ 9.95	=$	________
Listen UP, Leader!	____ copies X	$ 9.95	=$	________
Manager's Communication Handbook	____ copies X	$ 9.95	=$	________
I Wish You Would Just...	____ copies X	$ 9.95	=$	________
Manager's Communication Toolkit *(Includes all of the books above)*	____ copies X	$ 49.95	=$	________
The Leadership Secrets of Santa Claus	____ copies X	$ 14.95	=$	________
	Product Total		$	________
	*Shipping & Handling		$	________
	Subtotal		$	________
	Sales Tax:			
(Sales & Use Tax Collected on TX & CA Customers Only)	Texas Sales Tax – 8.25%		$	________
	CA Sales/Use Tax		$	________
	Total (U.S. Dollars Only)		$	________

*Shipping and Handling Charges

No. of Items	1-4	5-9	10-24	25-49	50-99	100-199	200+
Total Shipping	$6.75	$10.95	$17.95	$26.95	$48.95	$84.95	$89.95+$0.25/book

Call 972.243.8863 for quote if outside continental U.S. Orders are shipped ground delivery 7-10 days. Next and 2nd business day delivery available – call 888.822.9255.

Name________________________ Title________________________

Organization________________________

Shipping Address________________________

City________________________ (No PO Boxes) State____________ Zip ________

Phone________________________ Fax________________________

E-Mail________________________

Charge Your Order: ❑ MasterCard ❑ Visa ❑ American Express

Credit Card Number________________________ Exp. Date____________

❑ Check Enclosed (Payable to The WALK THE TALK Company)

❑ Please Invoice (**Orders over $250 ONLY**) P.O. Number (required)________________

Accts. Payable Contact________________________ Phone________________

WALK THE TALK®

PHONE
1.888.822.9255
or 972.243.8863
M-F, 8:30-5:00 Cen.

FAX
972.243.0815

ON-LINE
www.walkthetalk.com

MAIL
WALK THE TALK Co.
2925 LBJ Fwy., #201
Dallas, TX 75234

Prices effective November 2005 are subject to change.

No margin, no mission!

– **Sister Irene Kraus**
former president
Daughters of Charity National Health System

on "no win" situations

Ever feel like you just can't win no matter what you do? Me too! And there's no question it's a lousy feeling. Perhaps you sometimes feel that way as a result of dealings with me. If that's the case, I acknowledge my responsibility to correct it, because everyone deserves the opportunity to win. But you may not realize that you sometimes make me feel the same way. You occasionally deny me the opportunity to be a winner. And that's equally wrong.

As a manager, I've had my share of "damned if you do and damned if you don't" experiences – especially when it comes to making changes for the better. For example: Let's say you feel I have not adequately recognized your years of service in the past. So you're upset over something you feel I *haven't* done ... something you feel I should change. But the fact is I DO appreciate your loyalty, so I arrange a small celebration that everyone seems to enjoy – including you. Two days later, I ask you to work an extra shift because someone resigned. And I hear that you think I was just buttering you up to get you to work more; you feel the celebration was a manipulative sham. Now you're upset that I've *done* the thing you wanted in the first place. Result: I lose no matter what. That really hurts! And I begin to wonder: Why bother at all? Why try? I'm only human, and eventually I may stop trying altogether ... and probably get damned even more.

Look, no one gave me a magic wand or a manual on how to be the perfect boss. I admit I don't have all the answers. But I assure you I have the best of intentions. I'm doing the best I can to do right by EVERYONE – our patients and our staff. But I need your cooperation. I need your trust. And I sure would appreciate you occasion-ally giving me the benefit of the doubt.

The only thing worse than losing is being denied the chance to win. Think you're the only one who faces "no win" situations? Walk awhile in *my* shoes.

on selection and promotion

Speaking of "no win" situations ...

When it comes to selecting people for promotions, special assignments, and the like, it's tough to win. Tough, that is, if I pay any attention to what the candidates (and their friends) think.

Here's the scenario: Ten people are competing for one promotion. No matter whom I choose, one person is going to feel I made the right decision, and the other nine are gonna think I screwed up. If *you're* the one who gets selected, you'll probably suggest that I pay no attention to what the others think. Of course, if you *aren't* selected, you'll undoubtedly question my motives in making a selection that so many people think is wrong. Get the picture?

There's *a lot* more to selection decisions than you might think. Sometimes it may seem to you that I merely pick the people I like. Well, here's a shocker for you: It's true! But who I "like" is determined by weighing many factors, such as clinical expertise, technical skills, people skills, what we need now, what we'll need in the future, past performance, seniority, diversity considerations, flexibility, attitude, and much more. You don't have to use those same criteria in determining who *you* like.

So, if you're ever tempted to second guess my selection and promotion decisions, remember this simple fact: Nobody can do this job alone, so I need to create a solid team I can work with and depend on. There's no way I'd select someone I didn't feel could handle the job. To do otherwise would be just plain stupid on my part, and would create headaches for all of us down the road.

When it comes to selection and promotion, take *my* shoes ... please!

It is better to light one small candle than to curse the darkness.

– Confucius

on complaints and criticism

Call them complaints, criticisms, gripes, or just things that tick you off. We all have them ... they're just part of life. But when the number and frequency of these "issues" are so great that they become the predominant tone of our workplace, there's a problem. Excessive complaining and finger pointing not only make for a truly unpleasant atmosphere, but they also compromise our ability to provide high-quality healthcare. They exist more than we'd like to admit, and that bothers me. It *really* bothers me!

Believe me, I understand that working here means facing many challenges, competing priorities, staffing issues, shrinking resources, and ever-increasing time demands. I understand because I feel those same things myself. Fact is, we work in a challenging industry. But I've found that helping our patients, as we do, makes facing those challenges worthwhile. My guess is that, deep down inside, you understand that as well as I do.

Here's something else I understand: How we respond to challenges is our choice. We can choose to make the best or the worst of any situation. It's our call ... and we must take responsibility for our choices. Choosing a negative response – like griping and complaining to co-workers or patients – accomplishes nothing more than adding to the number of people who share your displeasure. And it makes things twice as hard for me. I not only have to be concerned with the issues that produce your concern, but I also must deal with the fallout of poor morale that results from "misery loves company" complaining.

So the next time you're tempted to react to a situation with nothing more than destructive criticism, please fight the feeling. You really do owe it to your patients and co-workers – and to yourself – to adopt as much of a "can do" attitude as possible. And come to me so we can work on, and hopefully fix, these issues together.

Think you're the only one challenged here? How'd you like to face our healthcare challenges *plus* the overlay of complaints and criticism? Try walking awhile in *my* shoes!

I never did
give anybody hell.
I just told the truth
and they thought
it was hell.

– Harry S. Truman

on dealing with performance problems

Everyone's got something they can point to as the absolute worst part of their job. This is mine. Addressing employee performance problems is a "necessary evil" of management. I hate it ... it takes a definite toll on me.

Maybe you sometimes think I jump on employees who have problems the first chance I get. Well, I admit I'm not perfect. Perhaps I have reacted too quickly on occasion. But, truth be told, I have a greater tendency to put those situations off as long as I can. Sometimes I've avoided confronting problems at all costs – that is, until they became so serious that I had no choice. Whether you've been the employee with the problem or the team member who has worked next to someone with an unaddressed performance discrepancy, my failure to act has been unfair to you. And for that, I apologize. My only explanation for this is that I'm human.

When facing an employee performance problem, I tend to experience two emotions: anxiety and anger. The anxiety comes from just thinking about what I have to do. I don't like telling someone they're not cutting it any more than you would. My guts churn; I get edgy; I have trouble sleeping. I want to put it off *and* get it over with as soon as possible – all at the same time. And then I get angry. I didn't create the problem; the employee did. He or she didn't live up to their responsibilities, and because of that, I have to go through this discomfort. Yet when I meet with the person, I'm supposed to be calm and businesslike, and follow a ton of guidelines that ensure I handle the issue consistently and fairly. I accept that responsibility, but trust me, there's nothing easy about it! Just once, I'd like people to understand and appreciate how tough this is on *me*.

Think you'd handle performance problems any differently if you were the manager? Have definite ideas on what I should or shouldn't do? Try walking awhile in *my* shoes!

on "being in on things"

Nobody tells me nothin'. I just work here!

Hey, I remember what it felt like to be a mushroom – kept in the dark and occasionally fed fertilizer. Because I remember, and because you're an important member of our team, I really am trying to keep you in the information loop. But honestly, you don't always make it easy.

You probably don't realize it, but often times I get more than my share of flack when I try to keep you and your co-workers informed. And that's not much of an incentive to keep the information flowing. If, for example, I mail something to your house, I hear complaints about wasting money on postage. Well you know what? I happen to feel that you're worth a stamp, or two, each year.

I try to schedule regular meetings with you, but you say you're too busy to attend. I send out memos that you sometimes brush aside ... and then later claim you never received. I give annual reports and other special briefings, around the clock, that you either miss or attend begrudgingly. The notices I post on bulletin boards aren't always read (even though the cartoons right next to them always *are*). And after all these efforts, and many others like them, I still hear ... you guessed it ... "Nobody tells me nothin'. I just work here." That's unbelievably frustrating. I really need your help with this one.

Keeping you "in on things" takes both of us. My part involves making sure that information is available to you. And if I fail to do that, you need to call me on it. Your part entails paying attention to the information – making an effort to use and absorb it in order to stay informed. If you choose not to do that, so be it. But please don't turn around and accuse me of keeping you in the dark.

Believe me, I *do* know that you work hard and that you're busy most (if not ALL) of the time. That's why I use so many different ways of communicating. And please know this: I'm committed to doing an even better job of keeping everyone "in the know" – regardless of the negative reactions I may receive.

Think keeping employees informed is easy? Try walking awhile in *my* shoes!

on being "objective, consistent, and fair"

In healthcare, a lot of us managers have come up through the ranks. I remember back when I used to sit in the lounge with you and participate in that great pastime: complaining about the boss. Well, now the boss is ME ... and I suspect that now I'm occasionally the subject of "lounge lament."

Now that I'm walking full time in my old boss's shoes, I've come to understand and appreciate a basic fact about management: **It's tough to supervise your friends.** If you've ever been placed in a lead worker position, I'm sure you know exactly what I mean.

"Bosses" inevitably must do things that don't mix well with friendship. Whether it's confronting work problems, doing performance evaluations, or even giving recognition, it's difficult to be objective and fair when dealing with a pal. The more distasteful the task, the greater the likelihood that I'll feel forced to choose between doing my job and keeping a friend. That's a heavy burden for anyone to carry. Making the "right" choice isn't as easy as it might seem.

Equally difficult is meeting the expectation that I be "consistent" and "fair" in my dealings with you. You expect both, and so do *my* bosses. Therein lies the dilemma. **Consistency** basically means treating everyone the same, while **fairness** means treating everyone the way they deserve to be treated based on their particular circumstances. So, since few situations I face are exactly alike, if I'm 100% consistent with everyone, I will inevitably be unfair to someone. And if I'm 100% fair with everyone, I'm consistent with no one; I end up treating people differently. No matter which way I go, somebody's gonna gripe. The best I can do is to simply do the best I can ... and somehow try to strike some balance between the two. I work on it every day. Welcome to my world!

Want to know how much easier it is to say "objective, consistent, and fair" than it is to be them? Walk awhile in *my* shoes.

If I had done everything I'm credited with, I'd be speaking to you from a laboratory jar at Harvard.

– Frank Sinatra

on how you perceive me

Someone once said, "If you want to be liked, don't become a manager." They were right! You just can't please everyone. If I've learned anything, it's that no matter what I do, inevitably somebody's gonna be steamed. That's a reality that comes with the job, and I accept it. But there's another reality I'd like you to know about and consider – a reality that comes with being human: I *care* what you and others think of me. I care a lot.

I got into healthcare because I wanted to help people. So, yes, it bothers me when you question my commitment to patients, to quality, and to you. Granted, I may not always communicate well enough for you to understand why I make the decisions I do. But please don't jump to conclusions. Providing high-quality patient care is always first with me. And right next to that are keeping people employed in a successful enterprise and ensuring our future in the community.

I especially care what you think about me when it comes to honesty, integrity, and fairness. I'll bet you consider yourself a fair person. You probably take pride in that. Well, so do I. But occasionally I get a bum rap for being unfair in my dealings with employees. You hear one side of the story – without all the facts – and form an opinion about me. I know it and it bothers me, but I can't defend myself because the facts are usually confidential. So I take the rap ... and maybe pretend I don't care. But I do.

I fully understand that I must earn your trust and respect, just as you must earn mine. And I'm working to do that. As I work on it, maybe you could give me the same benefit of the doubt that you would wish from me.

Before you judge me, try walking awhile in *my* shoes!

**Real joy comes
not from ease or riches
or the praise of men,
but from doing something
worthwhile.**

– Pierre Coneille

on the joys of the job

Before you go assuming this book is nothing more than a "woe is me" chronicle, let me set the record straight. There are plenty of joys that come with being a manager. Here are just a few of the "turn-ons" that make the job satisfying for me:

- Watching patients leave us healthier and happier than when they arrived.
- Making it easier for you to get your job done by implementing new procedures and technologies.
- Making a contribution – feeling that things came out differently and better because I was involved.
- Attending civic and association meetings, and bragging – with great pride – about the commitment and quality of our health-care team.
- Reflecting on past actions and decisions with the belief that I did the right thing … no matter how uncomfortable it might have been at the time.
- Receiving (and passing along) feedback from patients and their families, praising YOU – no matter if you're in admitting, labs, nursing, radiology, dietary, pharmacy, therapy, administrative support, housekeeping, or another of the all-important functions that come together to create our health-care experience.
- Achieving an adequate balance, as best I can, between my job and my personal life.
- Finding out from others that you think I'm a decent boss and, more important, a decent human being.

When it comes to the above, I'm guessing you experience many similar pluses. If so, you've *already* walked awhile in *my* shoes.

on "the future"

The Buddhists tell us to "plan as if you'll live forever, but live like today is your last." And that's pretty much what I'm trying to do – professionally and personally.

Sure, I have my personal plan all set for the moment I win the lottery: Living out the rest of my life in the lap of luxury. Yeah, right! In my more rational moments, however, I find myself looking *forward* with both excitement and anxiety. And that's especially true when it comes to my job.

My excitement stems from the belief that the future will produce many more opportunities for me (and you) to learn and grow, and to achieve the fulfillment we all seek. My anxiety comes, as it does for so many others, from the fear of the unknown.

The healthcare model has changed dramatically over the past several years, and I believe the pace of change will not only continue, but perhaps even accelerate. So, in the absence of a crystal ball, my professional plan for the future is simple: **Focus on the patient.** I'm going to keep asking myself, "What's best for our patients?" and let that question be my compass on this journey into the unknown. I encourage you to do the same.

Am I nervous about what lies ahead? You bet! Do I have all the answers? Absolutely not! In fact, I usually have more questions than answers. I'll be feeling my way along just like you will. I do, however, know this: The past is gone. The future is all that's left.

Anxious about the future? You're not alone. Walk awhile in *my* shoes.

what I ask of you ...

empathy

Appreciate the fact that my work is no **E**asier than yours. I face my share of challenges and occasional frustrations, too. Tasks often look easier than they are ... especially when somebody else has to do them.

Don't assume the worst of **M**e. *You* don't wake up in the morning asking, "How can I make life miserable for someone today?" Well, neither do I. If you have a problem with something I've done (or haven't done), talk to me about it instead of talking to others.

Continue to **P**erform your job as best you can – remembering that all of us are here to serve our patients in one way or another. That will make it easier for me to do the same.

Adopt the mindset that we both have tough jobs ... and for us to be successful, you need me as much as I need you.

Assume half **T**he responsibility for our working relationship. If we work well together, take half the credit. If we don't, accept half the responsibility for making it better.

Remember that I'm **H**uman. Before you judge me or decide how you'll deal with me, walk awhile in *my* shoes.

If **Y**ou do, I think you'll find ...

with more
understanding,
we can meet
in the middle
and walk
the rest of the way
TOGETHER.

Do not judge
any man
until you have walked
two moons
in his moccasins.

– Native American saying

The WALK THE TALK® Company

To order additional copies of this handbook or for information on other WALK THE TALK® products and services, contact us at

1.888.822.9255

or visit our website at

www.walkthetalk.com

Walk Awhile In *MY* Shoes – Healthcare Edition

Inquiries regarding permission for use of the material contained in this book should be addressed to:

The WALK THE TALK Company
2925 LBJ Freeway, Suite 201
Dallas, Texas 75234
972.243.8863

WALK THE TALK books may be purchased for educational, business, or sales promotion use.

Printed in the United States of America
10 9 8 7 6 5 4 3 2

Edited by Juli Baldwin and Jill Mason
Printed by MultiAd

ISBN 1-885228-43-0

walk awhile in *my* shoes

healthcare edition

gut-level, real-world messages
from employees to managers

Kathy Rice and Eric Harvey

The Authors

Kathy Rice, RPh., MBA, began her career as a staff pharmacist and currently serves as Chief Operating Officer of South Pointe Hospital – a member of the Cleveland Clinic Health System. In her 23 years at that location, she has successfully navigated her way through six job titles, three mergers, and four different hospital names. Kathy is very active in the community through Board memberships and serves as the president of the local Chamber of Commerce.

The authors dedicate this book to the outstanding people they have been privileged to work with and learn so much from.

Eric Harvey, President and CEO of the WALK THE TALK® Company, is an internationally known author, speaker, and educator in the areas of values-based business practices and organizational change. He has written twenty highly acclaimed books, including the best-selling *WALK THE TALK ... And Get The Results You Want*. With over 30 years of professional experience, Eric has held senior-level positions in numerous industries – including healthcare management.

The Publisher

Since 1977, The WALK THE TALK® Company's clear mission has been to help individuals and organizations achieve success through values-based business practices.

Besides offering an extensive library of cost-effective handbooks like this one, we specialize in providing training, consulting, and keynote presentations – all *customized* to your culture and business objectives.

Like more information? Contact our Professional Services group at **1.888.822.9255** or e-mail us at walkawhile@walkthetalk.com.

The Messages

Dear Manager:

I am every employee, and I work in every part of this organization. My collar is blue, pink, and white – frequently stained with the sweat of hard work ... and sometimes tears.

I am man, and I am woman. I'm every color, every belief, and every size. I'm old, young, and everything in between. I've worked here longer than you and not as long as you. I am a daughter. I am a son. I'm married and single, a parent and without children. I'm alone, and I'm surrounded by people I care about deeply.

Sometimes you may think of me only as a number, or perhaps just another small cog in a very large wheel that you have to manage. But like you, I am a human being filled with joys, fears, frustrations, and hopes. I feel, and I laugh, and I hurt. And, like you, I want to be understood, accepted, and appreciated.

The following pages are about opening up to you – about sharing my feelings on just a few of the many aspects of my job and how they affect me. Some of what you read may surprise you … some may bring a laugh or two. All of these pages, I hope, will encourage you to see me in a new, and perhaps much different, light.

I ask that you receive these messages with the same level of compassion and understanding that you wish from me as I read the flip side of this book. Chances are we're not as different as you may think. And just maybe, you'll be more inclined to "meet me in the middle," where we can begin a new and better working relationship.

Hear me. Understand me.

Walk awhile in *my* shoes.

It's not so much
that we're afraid of change
or so in love with
the old ways, but it's that
place in between
that we fear ... it's like being
between trapezes.
It's Linus when his blanket
is in the dryer.
There's nothing to hold on to.

– Marilyn Ferguson

on "change"

Okay, I admit it. When it comes to change, my first thoughts tend to be pretty self-centered: What about me? Will I have a job? Will it be the same job? Will I still be able to work with my friends? Will I be able to handle the new demands and challenges facing all of us in healthcare? Will I still be able to get satisfaction from what I do? What's the secret plan ... the hidden agenda? What? You don't have a plan? YIKES! No wonder I'm stressed.

Change is particularly tough on me because when it comes "rolling downhill," guess who's usually standing at the bottom of the hill? Me! I'm rarely the "decider," but almost always the "doer." Seems like I no sooner get comfortable and proficient with my job and WHAM! – a whole new set of requirements, protocols, and expectations are dropped on me. I *do* like feeling that I'm helping our patients and making a contribution to this organization. But, to be perfectly honest, it's getting harder and harder to feel that way.

Like you, I'm learning that life and continuous change are one and the same. But some changes are a lot easier to swallow than others. I'm basically okay with doing things differently to keep up with advancements in patient care – even though I question the "bureaucracy" that frequently comes with them. But I do resent those changes that are sometimes required because you screwed up or didn't think things through. Maybe if you asked my opinion a little more often, that wouldn't happen.

My biggest problem with change comes when you don't take the time to explain ***why***! If you know why, tell me, and you'll increase the odds that I'll support what has to be done. If you don't know why, ***try to find out***! And then let me know.

I'm struggling with this new healthcare environment of ours. I'm doing the best I can, but I'm scared. A little more sensitivity and patience on your part would go a long way toward helping me cope.

Change may not be easy for you, but at least you're calling some of the shots. Try walking awhile in *my* shoes!

We're in the caring business. But lately it seems like all the emphasis is on the business part – with the caring part left to us to figure out.

– Anonymous R.N.

on caring for patients

Of all the aspects of my job, this is the area that I have the strongest feelings about. And I can pretty much sum up those feelings by stating that, far too often, I feel that I provide quality patient care in *spite* of what happens here rather than *because* of it. It seems that everywhere I look, I find obstacles popping up between me and our patients. Obstacles ... and a lack of true support for what I'm expected to do. And I must admit, right or wrong, I frequently associate those obstacles with YOU – with things you have done or failed to do.

My biggest concern has to do with staffing. More accurately, it's the *lack* of staffing. Whether it's the need to cut costs or just the national shortage of healthcare workers (pharmacists, nurses, rad techs, and med techs, to name a few), I end up having to work extra shifts and literally run to get all the work done. It's getting harder and harder to spend those few extra minutes with each patient – giving them the extra TLC that brings your statement, "The patient comes first," to life.

Then there's the paperwork. "Make sure you get your charting done (but watch the overtime)." I got into this profession to care for people. But lately, I spend almost as much time *recording* what I do as *doing* it! It's always one more chart, one more form. And as I write, I hear: "But don't forget the patient. And remember to attend that in-service." No wonder I go home exhausted!

And of course, there's the issue of broken or antiquated equipment – a complete universe unto itself. From patient beds with missing pieces; to "user-friendly" computers that aren't so friendly and always seem to be "down"; to a simple shortage of supplies; I'm always having to work around one thing or another.

Look, maybe these obstacles (and a lot more like them) aren't of your choosing any more than they are of mine. But that doesn't make them any less tough on me. I need you to work even harder to make it possible for me to provide the quality care that you like to preach and brag about. And the first step in doing that is to walk awhile in *my* shoes.

on "no win" situations

Ever wrestle with the question: "How do I motivate my employees?" Well, I've got a suggestion I think will help. STOP TRYING! Instead, spend your time getting rid of the things that *de*-motivate me. And one of the top items on that list is "no win" situations.

If you've ever felt like you just can't win no matter what you do, you know what a downer that is. And it's something I experience more often than you might think. The plain fact is that there are times when I do what I'm supposed to do, and BOOM – I get nailed for it.

You keep telling me that nothing is more important than taking care of our patients. And I agree. So when I see a lost and rather nervous out-patient, I escort her to where she's supposed to go, rather than just pointing the way or giving a bunch of "turn left, then right, then right again" instructions. But guess what? Somebody reports me for being away from my work area, and BOOM – I'm in hot water.

Then there are times when I get punished for *good* performance. I bust my tail and do a good job handling tough tasks or problems, while some of my peers are goofing off or doing just enough to get by. So what happens the next time there's a tough job? I get stuck with it. BOOM, I lose again. And if I happen to screw up that next tough job? You guessed it: *KA*-BOOM!

I know (at least, I hope) that these actions are unintentional on your part. But that doesn't diminish the level of frustration I feel. I want to do a good job, and I want to win when I do. If I face too many "no win" situations, I'll eventually stop trying to win. Then, BOOM, we *both* lose.

Please think about this. Please walk awhile in *my* shoes.

The WALK THE TALK® Company

Since 1977, The WALK THE TALK Company has helped organizations achieve success through Ethical Leadership and Values-Based Business practices. And we're ready to do the same for you!

Through keynote and conference presentations, customized training and consulting, and high-impact publications like ***Walk Awhile In* MY *Shoes: Healthcare Edition,*** we have become one of the world's most respected providers of Ethics and Values-Based Business Resources.

To learn more about The WALK THE TALK Company, visit our website at: **www.walkthetalk.com**.

The WALK THE TALK team of professionals can help you bring important concepts like Leadership, Ethics, Communication, Recognition, and Customer Service to life with our customized training and presentations. From skill-building workshops to dynamic and energizing keynotes, we'll take your people 'beyond the book' to the next level of business success.

Call us today at **1.888.822.9255** or visit our website at **www.walkthetalk.com**.

WALK · THE · TALK®

Recommended Resources for Additional Study

Walk Awhile In* MY *Shoes – The original edition of this evolutionary handbook helps you break down *we vs. they* beliefs and behaviors that exist between "bosses" and "workers." OVER 1 MILLION IN PRINT! — $9.95

175 Ways To Get More Done In Less Time – This handbook is packed with 175 tips to help you get things done faster so you can accomplish more of your long-term goals. — $9.95

136 Effective Presentation Tips is a powerful handbook providing 136 practical, easy-to-use tips to make every presentation a success! — $9.95

Listen UP, Leader! – Ever wonder what your employees think about their leaders? This book tells you the seven characteristics of leadership that people will follow. — $9.95

The Manager's Communication Handbook – This powerful handbook will allow you to connect with employees and create the understanding, support and acceptance crucial to your success.— $9.95

I Wish You Would Just… – Two books in one! One side surfaces issues managers want their employees to hear while the other side includes messages from employees to their managers. — $9.95

Or ... for only $49.95, order **The Manager's Communication Tool Kit**
Containing all of these powerful books

Sometimes I feel like I'm standing at the corner of WALK and DON'T WALK!

– Unknown

on performance evaluations

From my perspective, both the *best* and the *worst* thing about performance evaluations is that they usually happen only once a year. Why best? Because they tend to be tedious and sometimes painful processes – similar to annual trips to the dentist. Why worst? Because all too often, they're the *only* time I get any detailed feedback on how well I am (or am not) doing. And sometimes even that doesn't happen constructively.

Evaluations represent "scaryland" for me because they're so *subjective*. Your opinion is going to affect my future. And there are no guarantees that one evaluator (and most of the time it is just *one* evaluator) really knows my job and how well I do it. So I often worry that my rating will be based solely on how much you like me. I worry you'll forget the good and remember only the bad. And I worry that my input won't be considered in the process.

Hey, I understand that performance evaluations probably aren't the most favorite part of your job. But they *are* important to me ... I've got a lot riding on them. If all you can do is call it like you see it, then please make sure you look hard enough to see the true picture.

And as you're looking, please remember that, just like you, I don't like negative surprises. Tell me throughout the year how I'm doing so I have time to work on things and so I'll know what to expect at evaluation time. Talk to me! Don't include something on my rating that I did six months ago unless you said something about it then. That's not fair. The way I see it, my evaluation should be a summary of your past feedback, NOT the first time I hear about where I'm strong and where I need to improve. And one more thing: How about getting my input before putting pen to paper? Ask me how I think I'm doing. Ask me about any obstacles I face. Ask me about things I do that I feel you don't know about. Ask me how I evaluate myself ... and why.

Have strong feelings about performance evaluations? Think they're a pain in the rear? Walk awhile in *my* shoes!

on loyalty

Hey, I read the papers and watch the evening news. I see what's happening in healthcare: "restructuring," "cost-cutting," "mergers," "labor shortages" on one hand; "downsizing" on the other. I see many of those trends here, and they scare me half to death. I've devoted one year, five years, or maybe thirty-five years to this organization, and sometimes I hardly recognize it anymore. And it seems like I'm either worrying if I'll still have a job, or wondering if it's really worth it for me to stick around. Too often, I'm either questioning your loyalty to me or my loyalty to you. That's not good.

Wanna know why I stay and don't jump ship? Well, it's not because of the money; the money here is okay, but there are places out there that will pay me just as much ... or more. And it's certainly not my schedule – which many times has me working off-shifts and holidays. Fact is, there are two things that keep me here: 1) the people I work with, and 2) those times when you have made me feel special ... when you've demonstrated loyalty to me.

With few exceptions, I really enjoy working with all of the people in my department. And I rely on you to help keep it that way. I need you to hold everyone accountable for doing their jobs. If someone (including me) isn't carrying their share of the load, you need to tell them (privately, of course) and make sure they do their part. Also, please avoid "playing favorites." It's really de-motivating to see one or two people get undeserved special treatment. One more thing: Consider creating opportunities for us to bond – especially if we've just gone through something traumatic like dramatic growth, downsizing, or a merger. Plan an informal get-together. Better yet, ask *us* to do it – for the whole department. Laughing together gives us a chance to blow off steam and get closer.

Finally, demonstrate loyalty to me, and I'll continue to reciprocate. You can start by recognizing my good work and years of service. And look for additional ways to show me that I'm appreciated. Do that, and I'm here for the long haul. After all, loyalty goes where loyalty is. You'll know that's true if you just walk awhile in *my* shoes.

The best mind-altering drug is *truth*.

– Lily Tomlin

on "being in on things"

Remember the childhood dig "I know something you don't know"? I remember it well. I learned at an early age that **knowledge is power**. And as I've grown up (or at least grown older), I've found that things haven't changed – especially at work. Now I frequently find myself thinking, "You know something I don't know." And that bothers me. It makes me feel like a kid again – in a negative sense.

Correct or not, my perception is that you know a lot more about our business than you're saying. I certainly understand that not all information is for public consumption. There are things that need to be kept confidential, like patient information or disciplinary actions. Even I have dealings with you that I don't want others to know about. But sometimes you display a parental "they don't need to know" attitude about non-confidential data. Worse yet, you either assume that "they don't want to be bothered with all this stuff," or you simply don't make the time to tell me what's going on in my department or with my job. And I end up feeling like the water boy rather than a member of the team.

Chances are I'm more interested in what's happening than you think. So when you get information – on our organization's performance, patient satisfaction, quality indicators, community needs assessments, financial data, etc. – pass it along. Let me know about plans for building expansions, adding new services, and yes ... even about another possible merger. Share information about our competition and trends in healthcare. And, you know, I really would like to attend those staff meetings and special briefings. But you need to give me more than fifteen minutes' notice that I can go. Maybe you could plan a little better so that everyone has a chance to hear the information.

And by all means, don't feel like you have to protect me from bad news. I'm an adult; I can take it. Sure, hearing bad news isn't pleasant, but it's no worse than being left in the dark ... and assuming the worst.

Do you sometimes feel like you don't know what's going on around here? Try walking awhile in my *even more* uninformed shoes!

on respecting my time

So much work, so little time! If you've ever felt that there's not enough time in the day to get your work done, you're not alone. I may not work long hours as frequently as you; and yes, I do sometimes take off as soon as my shift ends. But that doesn't make my time any less valuable than yours.

Despite the fact that we, in healthcare, are pretty darn good at "multi-tasking," I still haven't figured out how to be in three places at the same time ... or how in the world to get everything done "yesterday." But that sometimes seems to be your expectation nonetheless. The scenario is all too familiar: Somebody comes down on you because four patients just got discharged and their rooms need to be cleaned and prepped for some new admissions. And, of course, I'm expected to drop whatever I'm doing to get those rooms cleaned, "stat." I know it's important (as is most everything I have to do). And yes, I *do* believe that patients come first. But it sure is frustrating when every assignment you give me is "stat." Most times, you don't even ask what I'm in the middle of before you drop another top-priority job on me. Oh yeah, and you also want me to squeeze all my "routine" work in between those urgent tasks, too. It seems to me that when everything is "stat," eventually nothing is "stat."

Talk to me ... please! There are a lot of interruptions and urgent requests in our business, but ask me what I'm working on BEFORE you give me an assignment. That way I'll be much more likely to believe that you know my work is important ... and we can work together to "triage" those new tasks. Ask me if I have a few minutes to discuss how we are going to handle the situation instead of walking up and telling me what to do. I'll be much more inclined to believe that time is a precious resource that must be respected and used wisely. Act like my time isn't important, and I'll resent it. Even worse, I just might follow your lead.

Ever feel like your management time isn't always respected? Try walking awhile in my *employee* shoes!

**The best executive
is the one who has enough
sense to pick good people
to do what he wants done,
and self-restraint enough
to keep from meddling with
them while they do it.**

– Theodore Roosevelt

on resolving disputes

Call them complaints, grievances, disputes, whatever – the name really doesn't matter. Because I'm human, it's inevitable that I'll occasionally have concerns about how I'm treated. Sometimes my issues get resolved, or they work themselves out. But other times I just end up living with them. And I admit that it's hard for me to focus on caring for others when I'm not being heard. How my issues get resolved (or don't get resolved) plays a big role in how I view you ... and our organization.

I often hear the claim that we have an "open-door policy," where I can come to you to discuss my concerns "at any time." I appreciate the good intentions such a policy represents, but I don't think you realize how hard it can be to step through that door. Many times, you're just not accessible. I know how busy you are with budgets, doctors' concerns, going to meetings, preparing for certification surveys, and the like. But I need some of your time, too. For you, my issue may be just another problem you have to deal with. For me, it's a concern that's probably been bothering me for some time.

It's even more difficult to come to you when something *you* did (or didn't do) is the source of my concern. I have to go to the person who "done me wrong" in order to get resolution. Who wouldn't be uncomfortable with that? Who wouldn't fear being labeled a "troublemaker"? I know I could go and talk to HR, but sooner or later, I need to come to you. And who wouldn't fear the possibility of retribution? So, sometimes I just shut up (at least around you) and take it.

There's a catch-22 here that I don't know how to stop. You validly have a right to ask, "How can I possibly resolve employee complaints if I don't know they exist?" But I also must ask, "How can I be expected to use a process I fear – or at least have little confidence in?" Somehow, we've got to find a way, and the time, to talk things out. Please take the lead and help me find a way to effectively deal with my issues. After all, your success as a manager is ultimately linked to mine.

Think dispute resolution is a tough nut to crack? Try walking awhile in *my* shoes!

on participative management

All things considered, I feel I do a pretty decent job of managing my own life. I vote and I pay taxes. I obey the laws (most of them, anyway). I dress and feed myself – and probably others as well. I pay bills. I manage a checking account. I maintain a house or car (or both). I plan vacations. The list goes on and on. **I am a responsible adult with a brain!** But sometimes, at work, I'm treated like I can't think or be trusted to make good decisions. It happens more than you might think, and it bothers me as much as it would bother you.

Believe it or not, I do keep up with what's happening in the healthcare industry – and I *do* know that no matter how much we care for patients, like it or not, it's still a business. I also know that concepts such as "participative management," "empowerment" and "teams" are part of today's healthcare scene ... and that they can help us be successful in delivering high-quality patient care. Sometimes I see those trends happening in our organization; I see employees being given the opportunity to provide input on key decisions and new work processes. Sometimes, however, I don't – I don't see them happening, and I don't understand why.

Some of these trends may not be easy for you to accept and deal with. They probably aren't the way things were done when you came up through the ranks. And they may involve many hurdles that I'm not aware of and therefore can't truly appreciate. I just know that sometimes the chance to participate seems real, sometimes it's token, and sometimes it's nonexistent.

Here's what else I know: It's a lot easier to feel like an important part of this organization when I have the opportunity for meaningful involvement – especially when it comes to processes, protocols, and purchases in my area. Remember that I've got a stake in this organization's success just like you do. Ask for my input.

Even as a manager, have you ever felt that you'd like a little more say in how things are done around here? Try walking awhile in *my* shoes!

Like love, gratitude grows and multiplies with repeated use.

– Roberta L. Messner

on recognition

I've been known to say, "Forget the pats on the back – just put it in my check." Well, don't believe it. It's a crock! Regardless of how I may act, I *do* care a great deal about what you and others think of me and what I do. Recognition is important to me. That's why I wear award pins, t-shirts, and the like; that's why I display trophies in my home; that's why I hang certificates on my wall.

Believe it or not, I'm looking for more from this job than just a paycheck. There's got to be more, 'cause I'm sure not gonna get rich on what I make! What *do* I want? I want to feel good about myself and the work I do to help our patients and my co-workers; I want to feel like I really am an important part of this organization; and I want to know that *you* know I'm a valuable contributor. Stop by my work area occasionally – maybe on a holiday, when I've given up being with my loved ones to care for patients – and see me in action.

I fully realize that I don't do great work all the time. Some days I hit the bull's-eye, some days I'm in the outer rings, and every once in a while, I miss the target altogether. I don't expect you to see me as a "perfect performer" every minute of the day. But I do expect to be periodically recognized when I either go above and beyond the call of duty or just maintain good, solid performance over a long period of time. The more you recognize my good work, the more good work I want to do. It's funny the way that works. I think it's all part of "human nature."

I know you're often so busy you probably don't think about recognizing me. And maybe you sometimes figure you don't get recognition yourself, so why should you give it to others? But if you'll just make a greater effort to let me know you appreciate me, I'll do my best to reciprocate. And I promise I won't complain about receiving too much positive feedback!

Please understand how important this is to me. Walk awhile in *my* shoes.

Enjoyment is not a goal, it's a feeling that accompanies important ongoing activity.

– Paul Goodman

on the joys of the job

Before you go assuming this book is nothing more than a "woe is me" lament, let me set the record straight. There are many positive aspects about my job. Here's a list of just a few of the workplace "turn-ons" I experience:

- Knowing that I touched patients in some way and made their time with us a little better ... a little easier.
- Doing good work that I can be proud of ... and being recognized and appreciated for it – especially by YOU.
- Having my ideas on how to improve patient services taken seriously and occasionally adopted. I really like it when you ask, "What do you think?"
- Being part of a team in which everyone pulls together and carries his or her share of the load.
- Seeing behaviors, on your part, that indicate you not only care about patients, but you also care about ME.
- Having you trust my work ethic and competency enough that you don't feel the need to constantly look over my shoulder.
- Being respected as a good employee and, more important, a good person.
- Achieving an adequate balance between my job and my personal life.

When it comes to the above, I'm guessing you experience many similar positive feelings. If so, you've *already* walked awhile in *my* shoes.

Maybe we're not so different, after all.

on "the future"

I had a dream the other night. I was riding on a big sailboat in the middle of a huge storm. You were at the helm. We couldn't see the stars or any landmarks, and the radar wasn't working. Neither of us knew where we were headed – or if the boat would remain afloat. That dream pretty much sums up my view of "the future" around here.

All too often, as an employee, I feel like I'm just along for the ride. Sure, I do my part. I trim the sails, swab the deck, and bail water. But from where I'm sitting, I see the wheel in your hands. You may not know where we're headed any more than I do, but at least you're the one steering; you're the one with the most control.

Like most people, I look ahead with a certain amount of fear. I fear that I'll lose more than I'll gain. Are things going to change around here again? Will I have a job? The same job? Or will I have to go find something very different? Will I be able to maintain and improve upon the lifestyle I enjoy? Will there be health and happiness ahead? Will I be able to handle all the new challenges and requirements? Lots of questions ... very few answers.

I also look ahead with a great deal of hope. I hope that my fears will turn out to be unfounded – that things will be even better than they are now. Quality healthcare is important to society, and I want to be a part of making our community a great place to live, one patient at a time. It's hard work, but it's what I want to do. I just hope that creating a healthy community happens sooner rather than later.

What's most interesting about my dream is that you and I are in the same boat, sailing the same sea. It may be safer to stay in the harbor, but that's not what ships are built for. And that's not what *we're* here for. So I guess we'll keep sailing these seas together.

Please steer well. And every now and then, pull into port, step off the boat, and walk awhile in *my* shoes.

what I ask of you ...
empathy

Appreciate the fact that my work is no **E**asier than yours. I face my share of challenges and occasional frustrations, too. Tasks often look easier than they are ... especially when somebody else, like me, has to do them.

Don't assume the worst of **M**e. *You* don't wake up in the morning asking, "How can I make life miserable for someone today?" Well, neither do I. Give me the benefit of the doubt, and I'll do my very best to reciprocate. And please remember that I got into healthcare to play a part in helping people.

Continue to **P**erform your job as best you can. Be a role model for the commitment and quality you wish from me. And keep supporting those of us on "the front lines." Doing that will make it easier for me to do *my* job well.

Adopt the mindset that we both have tough jobs ... and that for us to be successful, you need me as much as I need you.

Assume half **T**he responsibility for our working relationship. If we work well together, take half the credit. If we don't, accept half the responsibility for making it better.

Remember that I'm **H**uman. Before you judge me or decide how you'll deal with me, walk awhile in *my* shoes.

If **Y**ou do, I think you'll find ...

with more
understanding,
we can meet
in the middle
and walk
the rest of the way
TOGETHER.